Baby animals in forest habitats

Bobbie Kalman

Crabtree Publishing Company

www.crabtreebooks.com

Created by Bobbie Kalman

For Summer-Lee Holly Kempt
Enjoy learning about these wonderful baby animals!

Author and Editor-in-Chief
Bobbie Kalman

Editors
Kathy Middleton
Crystal Sikkens

Design
Bobbie Kalman
Katherine Berti
Samantha Crabtree
(front cover)

Photo research
Bobbie Kalman

Print and production coordinator
Katherine Berti

Prepress technician
Katherine Berti

Photographs
BigStockPhoto: pages 7 (bottom), 19 (top),
    24 (bottom left)
Corel: pages 9 (bottom right), 10, 11, 13 (bear cub),
    17, 23 (middle right and top left)
Dreamstime: page 15 (bottom right)
Photos.com: pages 9 (top left), 15 (top),
    23 (top right)
Other photographs by Shutterstock

Library and Archives Canada Cataloguing in Publication

Kalman, Bobbie, 1947-
    Baby animals in forest habitats / Bobbie Kalman.

(The habitats of baby animals)
Includes index.
Issued also in electronic format.
ISBN 978-0-7787-7726-7 (bound).--ISBN 978-0-7787-7739-7 (pbk.)

    1. Forest animals--Infancy--Juvenile literature. 2. Forest
ecology--Juvenile literature. I. Title. II. Series: Kalman, Bobbie,
1947- . Habitats of baby animals.

QL112.K34 2011   j591.3'909152   C2010-907482-3

Library of Congress Cataloging-in-Publication Data

Kalman, Bobbie.
    Baby animals in forest habitats / Bobbie Kalman.
        p. cm. -- (The habitats of baby animals)
    Includes index.
    ISBN 978-0-7787-7739-7 (pbk. : alk. paper) -- ISBN 978-0-7787-7726-7
(reinforced library binding : alk. paper) -- ISBN 978-1-4271-9601-9 (electronic
(pdf))
    1. Forest animals--Infancy--Juvenile literature. 2. Forest animals--Ecology--
Juvenile literature. I. Title.
    QL112.K35 2011
    591.73--dc22

                                                2010047677

Crabtree Publishing Company

www.crabtreebooks.com   1-800-387-7650

Printed in China/022011/RG20101116

Published in Canada
Crabtree Publishing
616 Welland Ave.
St. Catharines, Ontario
L2M 5V6

Published in the United States
Crabtree Publishing
PMB 59051
350 Fifth Avenue, 59th Floor
New York, New York 10118

Published in the United Kingdom
Crabtree Publishing
Maritime House
Basin Road North, Hove
BN41 1WR

Published in Australia
Crabtree Publishing
386 Mt. Alexander Rd.
Ascot Vale (Melbourne)
VIC 3032

What is in this book?

What is a habitat?	4
What do they need?	6
What is a forest?	8
Helpful trees	10
Baby forest animals	12
Mammal mothers	14
Food in forests	16
Baby omnivores	18
A forest food chain	20
Fun in the forest	22
Words to know and Index	24

What is a habitat?

A **habitat** is a place in nature. Plants and animals live in habitats. They are **living things**. Living things grow, change, and make new living things.

This mother lynx is a living thing. It moves and has made babies.
The plants around it are also living things. They grow and make new plants.

4

chipmunk

plants

soil

rock

water

Non-living things

Habitats also have **non-living things**. The rocks, water, and soil in the picture above are non-living things. Living things need non-living things. Name two living things in the picture.

5

What do they need?

Living things need sunshine, air, water, and food. They find the things they need in their habitats. To stay alive, they need both non-living things and other living things.

This squirrel and chipmunk are eating the seeds of plants. Plants are living things.

Living and non-living

Some animals find homes under rocks or in **burrows**, or holes, in the ground. The ground and rocks are non-living things. Birds make nests in trees. They feed their babies worms or insects. Trees, worms, and insects are living things.

This baby wolf lives in a burrow under the ground.

burrow

What is a forest?

A forest is a habitat where many trees grow. Other plants grow in forests, too. Not all forests are the same. Some forests are in parts of the world where the weather is always hot. These forests are called **tropical forests**. In some tropical forests, it rains every day. These forests are called **rain forests**.

This baby margay lives in a rain forest.

Forests with four seasons

Some forests are in parts of the world where there are four **seasons**. The seasons are spring, summer, autumn, and winter. In each season, the temperature changes.

Spring is warm and rainy. Flowers bloom, and baby animals are born.

bobcat cub

Summer days are long and hot. It is a good time for babies to explore the forest!

baby chipmunk

In autumn, the leaves fall from the trees. Baby squirrels store food for the winter.

baby squirrel

Winters are cold, and the days are short. Baby animals find less food to eat.

cougar cub

Helpful trees

Baby forest animals need trees. They make their homes in trees. Some hide in trees to keep safe. In summer, trees shade the animals from the sun and keep them cool. Many forest animals also find food in trees.

This bobcat cub lives in a tree log. It is safe inside the log.

This mother and baby porcupine are eating the bark of a tree branch.

Birds make their nests in trees. This baby owl lives high up in a tree.

11

Baby forest animals

These are just a few of the baby animals that live in forests with four seasons. They are all the same kind of animal. Do you know which kind of animal they are?

red fox kit   baby squirrel

lynx cub   bobcat cub   cougar cub

What are mammals?

The animals on these two pages are all **mammals**. Mammals have hair or fur. How many legs do these mammals have?

baby chipmunk

bunny rabbit

raccoon kit

bear cub

deer fawn

wolf pup

Mammal mothers

Mammal mothers look after their babies. After they are born, they feed the babies milk from their bodies. Drinking mother's milk is called **nursing**. Most mammal mothers take good care of their young and keep them safe. How are these mothers taking care of their babies?

This red fox mother is feeding her kits milk. How many kits are nursing?

This mother cougar is taking her cub to a new home. Many mothers change the homes of their babies often to keep them safe. Cat mothers carry their babies like this.

Deer mothers hide their fawns to keep them safe from other animals.

Wolf pups nurse, but they also eat meat that their mother brings up from her stomach.

Food in forests

Some baby animals nurse for a while and then start eating the same food as their parents. They find the foods they need in their forest habitats. Some forest animals eat plants. Animals that eat mainly plants are called **herbivores**.

Baby deer eat grasses, small plants, and the leaves and branches of bushes.

Baby bunnies eat grasses, flowers, and weeds in the fields beside forests.

Baby carnivores

Carnivores are animals that eat other animals. Cougars, bobcats, wolves, and coyotes are carnivores. Some baby carnivores start learning how to hunt animals soon after they are born. Animals that hunt are called **predators**. The animals they hunt are called **prey**.

*This bobcat mother is teaching her cub how to look for animals to eat. Bobcats **stalk**, or sneak up, on their prey to catch it. They eat mainly rabbits and small deer.*

Baby omnivores

Omnivores are animals that eat both plants and other animals. They can find food more easily than herbivores or carnivores can because they eat more than one kind of food. Bears, raccoons, chipmunks, and mice are omnivores.

Bears eat plants, but they also eat fish, frogs, insects, and other foods they find. These brown bears are looking for fish to catch in a river beside a forest.

Foxes are omnivores. They prefer to eat other animals, but they will eat plants if they cannot find animals to hunt. This red fox kit has caught its first mouse.

Chipmunks eat plants and their parts, such as seeds, nuts, and berries. They also eat animals, such as small birds and their eggs, small frogs, worms, and insects.

A forest food chain

sun

energy

All living things need **energy**. Without energy, living things cannot move or grow. Energy starts with the sun. Plants use the sun's energy to make food. Animals get their energy by eating plants or other animals. Each time they eat, the sun's energy gets passed along to them. The passing of energy from one living thing to another is called a **food chain**.

1. Plants make food from sunlight. The sun's energy goes into the plants.

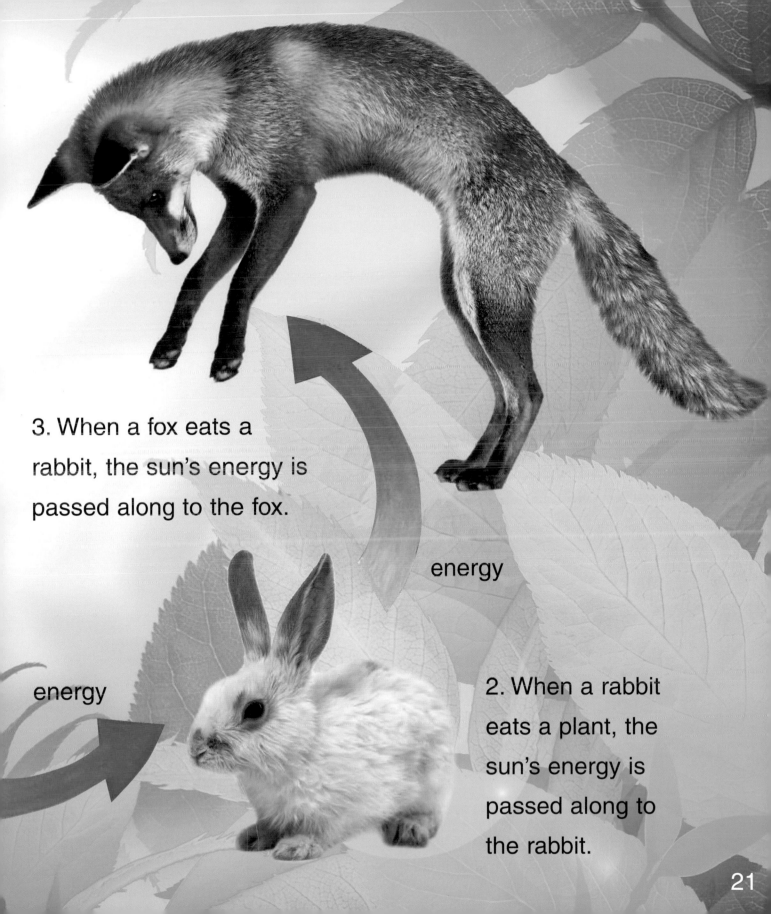

3. When a fox eats a rabbit, the sun's energy is passed along to the fox.

energy

energy

2. When a rabbit eats a plant, the sun's energy is passed along to the rabbit.

Fun in the forest

"Hi there! Welcome to our forest habitat. This is how we have fun. How do you have fun in your habitat?"

"We hang out with our friends."

"We wrestle each other for fun."

"We try new foods."

"We learn to talk."

"We play hide-and-seek."

"We learn to climb."

"We learn to fly."

"In winter, we play in the snow."

23

Words to know and Index

babies
pages 4, 7, 8, 9, 10, 11, 12–13, 14, 15, 16

birds
pages 7, 11, 19

carnivores (predators)
pages 17, 18

food
pages 6, 7, 9, 10, 14–15, 16–17, 18–19, 20–21, 23

food chain
pages 20–21

herbivores
pages 16, 18

Other index words
forest fun pages 22–23
habitats pages 4, 5, 6, 8, 16, 22–23
mammals pages 13, 14–15
mothers pages 4, 11, 14–15
nursing pages 14, 15, 16
omnivores pages 18–19
plants pages 4, 5, 6, 8, 16, 18, 19, 20–21
seasons pages 9, 12
trees pages 7, 8, 9, 10–11

homes
pages 7, 10, 11, 15

living things
pages 4–5, 6, 7, 20
(**non-living things**
pages 5, 6, 7)